Circle of
Catholic Women

~ *journal two* ~

Facilitator Guide

~

Karen Pavlicin

Juloya
celebrating life

✳ ✳ ✳ ✳ ✳ ✳ ✳ ✳ ✳
Woodbury, Minnesota

NIHIL OBSTAT: Reverend J. Michael Byron, Censor Librorum
IMPRIMATUR: The Most Reverend John C. Nienstedt,
                Archbishop of Saint Paul and Minneapolis
                March 6, 2010

The Nihil obstat and Imprimatur are official declarations that a book or pamphlet is free from doctrinal or moral error. No implication is contained therein that those who have granted the Nihil obstat and Imprimatur agree with the contents, opinions, or statements expressed.

Design by Andermax Studios.

ISBN-13: 978-1-934617-12-0 (pbk.)
Printed in United States of America.
 1 2 3 4 5 6 7 8 9 10

Juloya is an imprint of Elva Resa Publishing
8362 Tamarack Vlg Ste 119-106, St Paul, MN 55125
http://www.juloya.com, http://www.elvaresa.com
http://www.circleofcatholicwomen.com

Circle of Catholic Women journals are available through traditional bookstores, online, or direct from the publisher. Bulk discounts available. A portion of profits support outreach programs for women, children, and families.

Journal Two Facilitator Guide

Setting Up a Circle Program

Circle of Catholic Women is a journal series designed to prompt individual reflection and group sharing and discussion. The purpose is to deepen women's understanding of their faith and build fellowship with other women as they inspire each other to live their faith in all aspects of their daily lives.

This facilitator guide is specific to *Journal Two* in the series. Each journal can be used without a facilitator guide. The guide is meant to provide additional ideas and sample scripts to make it easier for facilitators to prepare for and lead group discussions or retreats. It is especially helpful for new facilitators or for situations where facilitators might change from session to session. The guide also includes ideas for parish leaders who are new to the circle program or who are just beginning to set up a women's circle in their parish.

Gathering women to your circle

If you already have a group of women ready to begin using *Circle of Catholic Women—Journal Two*, you can skip ahead to "setting up the format and facilitation of your circle" (p. 3). If you are just beginning

1

your circle program, here are some ideas for inviting women to participate in a circle.

- Talk with existing groups within your parish, such as faith formation, adult education, Bible study, or women's ministry. Is there a desire for more fellowship among women? For a deeper understanding of faith within the context of daily life? Form a small group of women from an existing spiritual or fellowship group in your parish.

- Print an invitation in your parish bulletin.

- Host an information table after weekend services. Display a copy of the journal and accept registrations.

- Mail or email an invitation to women who have participated in previous parish events.

- Print an article in your local newspaper if you'd like to invite women outside your parish to join your circle.

Here is a sample description of the program for an announcement:

Circle of Catholic Women
[Name of parish or women's ministry] is hosting a journaling and discussion series tailored to women seeking deeper spiritual connections and life balance. Join us as we journey with other women to grow closer to God. Through personal journaling and group sharing, we will explore personal prayer practices, rituals and traditions, relationships, spiritual role models, values and beliefs, and additional topics aimed at helping today's women deepen their faith and find peace within their daily lives. *Circle of Catholic Women—Journal Two* personal writing journals provided.

[Meeting information, for example: 8 weekly sessions beginning April 14. Tuesday mornings 9:30-11 a.m. at Saint Church. Childcare provided.]

To register please contact [coordinator name and phone number] by [deadline].

Setting up the format and facilitation of your circle

To prepare for your circle program, you'll want to consider the best time of year, format, schedule, and facilitation you have in mind for your program. For example, you might want to add the journaling program to an annual retreat, offer a four-week session following a Bible study program, or follow up a Lenten faith-sharing program with eight weeks of journaling. You might need to offer both a daytime and evening option depending on the ages and work schedules of your participants. Your planning might include daycare options, meeting room scheduling, enlisting facilitators, and other program details. As you begin planning, consider the following.

Time of year

Select a time of year for your circle program that fits into your parish's overall adult faith formation calendar. Even if your group will meet in homes or community venues separately from your church's programs, you'll want to be aware of other programs that might compete for your group's interest or conflict with your group's meeting times. For example, if your church has an established Bible study program during a particular month or a personal reflection or group sharing program during Lent, you might set up a schedule for your circle program following Easter or at the start of the school year. The circle program should complement other faith-sharing programs available to women in your parish. The time of year you select might also affect meeting room availability and options for length and format of your program.

Format and schedule of meetings

Your circle of women can choose to use the journal in a variety of settings. For example, you can select two journal topics for a half-day retreat, four topics for a month-long weekly series, or the entire journal in an eight-week session, with a weekly meeting on the same day and time each week.

Decide and communicate the format of your program. Write down your meeting dates and times. If you have a large group or enough

3

interest from women with different schedules, consider offering a simultaneous program during the day and in the evening, or a weekend retreat schedule.

Number of times our group will meet: _____

Intro/Gathering:

Date: _____ From: _____ AM/PM To: _____ AM/PM

Discussion Topic/Chapter:

Date: _____ From: _____ AM/PM To: _____ AM/PM

Discussion Topic/Chapter:

Date: _____ From: _____ AM/PM To: _____ AM/PM

Discussion Topic/Chapter:

Date: _____ From: _____ AM/PM To: _____ AM/PM

Discussion Topic/Chapter:

Date: _____ From: _____ AM/PM To: _____ AM/PM

Discussion Topic/Chapter:

Date: _____ From: _____ AM/PM To: _____ AM/PM

Discussion Topic/Chapter:

Date: _____ From: _____ AM/PM To: _____ AM/PM

Discussion Topic/Chapter:

Date: _____ From: _____ AM/PM To: _____ AM/PM

Discussion Topic/Chapter:

Date: _____ From: _____ AM/PM To: _____ AM/PM

Location of meetings

Decide where your group will meet. Select an environment conducive to conversation, prayer, and fellowship. Common choices include rooms at your church, a school, or a central location in your community. Circle discussions can also take place in homes, but be aware that some women might find hosting a meeting stressful, which might change the focus of some discussions.

Our group will meet at this location: _____

_____

Conveniences

What conveniences will your group need at this location? For example, is there a bathroom, an area to set up refreshments, ample parking, and room to sit or move around comfortably? Does your group need childcare? Your church or school might already have a childcare provider and place for children to play away from your meeting area. Teens preparing for confirmation, as well as volunteers from your women's ministry or parish, might be an option for caring for children. Be sure all volunteers have completed your archdiocese's background and training requirements for working with children.

Conveniences our group will need: _____

_____

Facilitation

Decide how your group discussions will be led. Depending on the size of your group, the personality of your participants, and your meeting surroundings, you might prefer to have a primary facilitator who organizes the meetings and leads the discussions. You might need a team of facilitators to lead several small group discussions. Or your group might prefer to have different volunteers sign up to facilitate each week or to have no formal facilitator.

Our group's lead facilitator or coordinator:

Name _____

Phone _____   Email _____

Notes about this person's role: _____

_____

Our group's additional facilitators:

Name _____

Phone _____   Email _____

Role: _____

Name _____

Phone _____   Email _____

Role: _____

Name _____

Phone _____   Email _____

Role: _____

Be sure to explain the facilitation process to your group ahead of time so everyone understands and is comfortable with the approach. When selecting facilitators, you'll want to look for someone who has the ability to create a welcoming atmosphere, is a good listener, and has a gentle but firm ability to redirect conversation and keep a group on task. General tips to share with facilitators are found in *Journal Two*'s introduction and include:

- Be prepared. Complete your own journaling and look over the discussion questions ahead of time.

- Set a positive and welcoming tone. Encourage everyone to let go of their distractions or other worries so they can fully engage in the present discussion. Invite all participants to share their experience, thoughts, and questions. Help each person feel welcome and encouraged to participate but not pressured.

- Review the guidelines for meeting as a group, such as keeping conversations confidential within the group in order to create a trusted environment. Ask everyone to be mindful that all sharing is personal and that each story should be honored and respected.

- Help keep the group reasonably on topic and on time. Guide the discussion and timing to cover all topics your group is expecting to talk about within the overall allotted time. If the discussion takes a slight tangent, go with it and see where the Spirit guides you. At the appropriate time, gently refocus the group back on topic.

- Listen without judgment. Remind participants that you aren't there to solve each other's problems, but to let each woman who wants to share be heard and to provide a supportive environment for that sharing. It's okay to acknowledge someone's joy or pain, but avoid advice or opinions. Listening is as important as being heard. Be open to silence. Be open to truly listening in a way that you may reflect on it later for your own growth and learning.

- If one person dominates a conversation or has trouble bringing her thoughts to closure, gently thank her for sharing and explain that due to time constraints, you'd like to invite others to share. As facilitator, remember that it is not your role to dominate either; you are there to guide the discussion and allow everyone who wants to share to have the opportunity to do so.

- Keep the conversation inspirational and respectful. Recognize that some topics will be fun while others may generate deep emotions. Be aware of times when someone may need a moment to collect her thoughts or composure. As facilitator, be sensitive to the potential need for a short break.

- About ten minutes before closing, let participants know you are near the end of the discussion time. Guide the group toward last reflections or comments before closing with a prayer. Thank everyone for participating and encourage them to reflect on this time spent together before beginning the next journal topic.

- Be open to suggestions for changes to the format or facilitation. What works well for one group may be different from what works for another.

Additional information for our group's facilitators based on the format we have chosen for our circle program:

_____

_____

_____

Initial gathering
Consider an informal gathering before you begin your program. This is especially helpful if the women in your group do not know each other, your parish has not offered a journaling program recently, you are beginning a weekend retreat and want an opportunity for everyone to meet each other the first evening, or you feel such a gathering will help ease anxiety or answer questions about the program.

If you decide to hold an initial gathering before the program begins, here are a few suggestions:

- Open with a fun ice-breaker that helps everyone get to know a little about the other women in the group.

- Hand out the journals if participants have not already received their copy.

- Take a few moments to look through the journal together.

- Talk about the schedule and format your group will use: how often you will meet; the dates, start and end times, and locations of meetings; and which topics you will cover (especially if you will discuss only some of the topics or in a different order). Consider giving participants a written agenda or calendar summarizing the schedule, format, location, and topics.

- Encourage participants to journal about the topic before the group meeting(s) so everyone can get the most from their time together.

- Point out in the journal's introduction the tips for personal journaling. These include:

  – Make two or three appointments with yourself during the week for quiet reflective time, in a place where you can read and reflect with few interruptions.

  – Be honest with yourself when you answer questions. Know that whatever you journal about, you have a choice whether or not you want to share it with the group.

  – You do not have to answer all of the questions. Write about what moves you, what you have questions about, what frustrates you or causes you to more deeply reflect on the impact of your faith on your daily life.

- Talk about how the group will be facilitated. Introduce the facilitator(s). Review the role of a facilitator so participants understand that this person's role is to help keep the group reasonably on topic and on time and to create a welcoming environment for everyone to share.

- Share general expectations for group discussions. Point out in the journal's introduction the tips for meeting as a group. Especially emphasize that this is a trusted circle and no one should share someone else's personal story or comments outside the circle without that person's permission. This helps ensure a safe place for everyone to share and grow.

- Go over logistics, rules, or courtesies related to your meeting environment, such as cell phone use, parking restrictions, clothing or footwear guidelines, location of bathrooms or other facilities, and childcare information.

- Answer questions. Help everyone feel comfortable that this will be a personally rewarding experience in an environment of compassionate trust.

The labyrinth

The cover of each journal incorporates a labyrinth; at the center is a circle, a special place of reflection and renewal. Walking a labyrinth is a journey of self-awareness, enlightenment, and peace. Unlike the maze of our daily lives with all its choices and unexpected turns, a labyrinth has only one path to the center and back. It allows us to completely focus and meditate and find our center.

If possible, see if your group can take a field trip to walk a labyrinth. Or consider creating one in your meeting room or incorporating a labyrinth into your discussions or environment.

Circle Discussions

Overview

The purpose of circle discussions is to gather women together to share thoughts, beliefs, questions, and stories about faith in their daily lives.

The personal journaling that takes place before the meetings prompts women to think about what they believe, how their faith has played out in their lives, and what they hope for the future. By voicing these reflections in a trusted environment, women come to better understand their own faith and its effect on their daily lives. Listening to other women share their stories offers new perspective, affirmation, and ideas. In addition to their own personal growth, participants often find new friendships and deeper spiritual connections with the other women in their circle and in other close relationships in their lives. Following are some suggestions for ways to create a trusted circle and a discussion environment that encourages and nurtures this spiritual growth.

Setting up the environment

For each meeting, you'll want to create an atmosphere that encourages spiritual connections, minimizes distractions, and makes it comfortable and easy for women to focus on participating in the circle. The physical setup of the room can help create this atmosphere.

Know ahead of time approximately how many women will attend the meeting. If you have fewer than eight to ten women, you can plan to have everyone sit in a circle of chairs or around one table with a candle in the center. If you have a group of 30 or so women, you can set up a gathering place for the beginning and ending of the meeting, where all of you can stand together in a circle around a candle on the floor or within a labyrinth. Then separately set up small gathering areas where groups of four to seven women can meet in a more intimate circle. You want a discussion environment that allows each person to see everyone else in the small circle and that allows each woman to have an opportunity to share.

Consider placing an object related to the day's discussion topic on the table or floor in the middle of your small circles.

Off to the side of the gathering circles, or near the entry of the room, set up a general utility table. This is a place to display things such as announcements, name tags and pens, resources, and refreshments. The utility table keeps these items out of the way of the circles but still close by.

Minimize distractions by closing the door to the room, moving children to a childcare room, and turning off cell phones. Set the lighting in the room to allow participants to see each other and what they have written in their journals.

General meeting format

In general, you'll want to follow a similar format for each meeting. This familiarity helps the group know what to expect and keeps the focus on the discussion rather than learning a new format. You can add variety by changing the table setting, the method of dividing into small groups, or the opening or closing activities or prayers. Following is the general suggested format.

- Have the room set up before participants arrive. As women arrive, ask them to put on name tags.

- Gather in a circle with all participants. Remind the group of the day's topic for discussion. Open with a prayer, poem, or music. You can use the opening provided in the journal or use a passage, poem, or song brought in by a member of your group.

- Depending on the size of your group and the topic of discussion, you might open the discussion in your large group by inviting everyone to share one thing that moved them about the journal topic or their experience since your last meeting.

- Form small circles for sharing. Sharing responses in more intimate small group conversations allows more women to share with each other and to develop close relationships. Facilitators should have guidelines before the meeting regarding questions you will discuss and the time allotted for the discussion.

- Gather back together as a larger group. If time permits, invite women to briefly share comments from their small group that might benefit everyone to hear. Use this time to mention resources, get feedback on the session, remind participants to reflect on this experience before beginning the next topic, make an announcement about upcoming activities, or other administrative tasks.

- Close with a prayer.

Encouraging friendships

To encourage friendships within the circle, set up ways for women to get to know each other and to connect before, during, after, and in between meetings. For example, at each meeting, have a theme for name tags; in addition to or in place of the suggested themes in the chapter-by-chapter guide, ask each person to write a favorite movie, book, or hobby on her name tag and sit near someone with similar

13

or opposite favorites. If you have a large group, use creative ways to select smaller discussion groups, such as drawing Uno cards and gathering in tables by card color. Encourage women to sit next to a different person each time you meet. At the beginning of each meeting, go around the large circle and share one thing about yourself that few people know about. Draw names after each meeting and later in the week call the person whose name you drew. Consider a social gathering with just the women or with their families a few weeks after the final session.

Other ideas for encouraging friendships in our circle:

_____

_____

_____

Leading discussions

Each chapter in the journal includes suggested discussion questions. You may use these questions or create your own. It helps participants to know ahead of time the primary topics or questions your group will discuss. Being able to prepare helps women think about the stories and ideas they'd like to share with the group; it also helps put their minds at ease if the topic is a difficult one for them.

When leading a circle discussion, don't rush between questions. Give the group time to answer and discuss. Plan the approximate amount of time you want to spend on each question given your overall allotted time for the discussion. The following pages offer a basic chapter-by-chapter script you might choose to follow for each meeting. You'll find conversation starter suggestions if needed. Use the workbook spaces and margins to make additional notes to plan for your discussion.

Chapter-by-Chapter Guide

Following is a chapter-by-chapter guide you can use or adapt to meet your group's needs. For your convenience, this guide includes the opening and closing prayers and discussion questions from *Journal Two*.

The suggestions in this section assume that participants have reflected on the topic and written in their journals before the meeting and that each chapter discussion is taking place on a different day as its own meeting. If your group will be covering more than one topic at a time, using the journal in a retreat setting, or if participants will not be writing about the topic prior to the meeting, please refer to the Retreats chapter (pp. 46-56) for additional ideas.

You might also want to add notes throughout this section to include ideas from the Circle Discussions chapter (pp. 11-14), such as ideas you liked for setting up the room or encouraging friendships.

Be sure to plan at least one meeting ahead in the guide so you can announce any changes to the group questions you'll discuss and ask women to bring in something special to share in the next meeting.

Connecting with God: Spiritual intimacy
& inspiration

Gather into a large circle.

Opening prayer
Leader: Today's discussion is about creating an intimate relationship with God and finding sources of spiritual inspiration.

Please join me in the opening prayer found on page 11 of your journal.

> Lord, I desire to be closer to you, to know you more intimately, and to love you fully and unconditionally. Guide me in my journey as I nurture and strengthen my relationship with you and with my loved ones. I will look for inspiration to renew and deepen my love for you, my trust in you, and my joy in giving you my all. Amen.

Announcements or questions for the large group:

_____

_____

Instructions for dividing into small groups or pairs:

_____

_____

Group discussion
Ideas for setting your circle table: Bible, prayer book, retreat brochures, examples of labyrinths and prayer gardens, books on intimacy. Name tag theme: one of your personal sources of spiritual inspiration.

What moved you about this topic?

Allotted time for group discussion: _____

Leader: Please refer to the suggested group questions on pages 22-23 in your journal. Before we begin our discussion, did anyone write down other questions or aspects of prayer you would like to talk about? We'll add as many of these topics as we can in our time together.

_____

_____

_____

Questions from *Journal Two* our group will discuss:

❐ What challenges or joys do you experience in your new and established relationships? How are these similar to what you experience in your relationship with God?

❐ What are some ways you nurture your relationships? How do you nurture your relationship with God the Father, Son, and Spirit?

❐ What would your ideal relationship with God be like? What are some ways you are inspired to work toward that relationship?

❐ What are your favorite sources of spiritual inspiration?

Other topics or questions our group will discuss:

_____

_____

_____

Gather in the larger circle.

Leader (optional): Would anyone like to share with us something particularly meaningful to you from your small group discussion?

Announcements, resources, reminders:

_____

_____

*Conversation starters:
Who are some of the
most important people
in your life?
What did you learn
about yourself while
journaling about this
topic? Was this topic
easy or difficult for you
to write about?*

17

Comments about upcoming sessions (such as changes to group discussion topics):

_____

_____

For next time, bring in something that represents a favorite personal ritual or routine that makes your day complete or bring examples or photos of your favorite regular activities with family or friends.

Other administrative items to share with the group:

_____

_____

Closing prayer

Leader: Thank you for sharing with us today. Please join me in saying the closing prayer on page 22 of your journal.

Lord, with all my heart and being I desire to be closer to you. Just as I care for my closest human relationships, I will make time to get to know you better, communicate more clearly with you, learn from you, trust you, and love you with all my heart. I will seek out sources of inspiration that help me bring the best I have to offer our relationship. Let me come closer, Lord, so I may share in your loving, intimate embrace for all eternity. Amen.

Rituals & Traditions: Personal rituals & routines

Gather into a large circle.

Opening prayer

Leader: Today's discussion is about personal rituals and routines, outward signs of love and affection, and spiritual routines that help us form positive, loving habits.

Please join me in reading the opening prayer found on page 25 of your journal.

> Father, each day I go about my life following routines, creating rituals, and sending signals about my love and affection to others. Teach me to be thoughtful and purposeful in the daily rituals that form my habits and actions. Help me make each thought and act loving and giving. Amen.

Other announcements or questions for the large group:

_____

_____

Instructions for dividing into small groups or pairs:

_____

_____

Ideas for setting your circle table: prayer book, daily planner, healthy menu, health and fitness magazines.

Ask women to bring something for the table that represents a favorite personal ritual or routine or examples or photos of favorite regular activities with family or friends.

Name tag theme: one of your personal daily or weekly rituals you feel good about.

Group discussion

Allotted time for group discussion: _____

Leader: Please refer to the suggested group questions on pages 33-34 in your journal. Before we begin our discussion, did anyone write down other questions or aspects of personal rituals and routines

19

you would like to talk about? We'll add as many of these topics as we can in our time together.

_____

_____

_____

Questions from *Journal Two* our group will discuss:

☐ What signs of love and affection do you most enjoy giving or receiving?

☐ What challenges, habits, or purposeful interactions come from your transition moments or your rules of the house?

☐ What are some of your favorite rituals with your family and friends? How have these brought you closer together? (Take time to share items or photos brought in.)

☐ How do your personal rituals and routines encourage or limit your spiritual growth?

Other topics or questions our group will discuss:

_____

_____

_____

Conversation starters: Would anyone like to share a good (or bad) habit you've developed from your personal daily rituals? What are some of your house rules? What do you find most challenging about the spiritual aspect of your day?

Gather in the larger circle.

Leader (optional): Would anyone like to share with us something particularly meaningful to you from your small group discussion?

Announcements, resources, reminders:

_____

_____

Comments about upcoming sessions (such as changes to group discussion topics):

_____

_____

Other administrative items to share with the group:

_____

For our next discussion, please bring a photo of your parents.

_____

Closing prayer

Leader: Thank you for sharing with us today. Please join me in reading the closing prayer on page 33 of your journal.

Lord, help me be thoughtful, purposeful, and loving as I choose my daily rituals and routines. May my habits bring me closer to you and the people I love most in my life. Amen.

Relationships: Parents

Gather into a large circle.

Opening prayer
Leader: Today's discussion is about our parents and how they've influenced our lives, and the parenting roles we now play as adults.

Please join me in reading the opening prayer found on page 37 of your journal.

> Lord, you give me the blessing and challenge of parenting relationships. Help me see the wisdom and love of my parents and to be a good guide and role model to all children you bring into my life. Help me be an example of your love, respect, and discipline as I bring the lessons of my childhood into my adult responsibilities in my home and community. May my parenting relationships enrich my life and the lives of those around me. Amen.

Announcements or questions for the large group:

_____

_____

Instructions for dividing into small groups or pairs:

_____

_____

Group discussion
Allotted time for group discussion: _____

Leader: Please refer to the suggested group questions on pages 47-48 in your journal. Before we begin our discussion, did anyone write down other questions or aspects of parent relationships you would

Ideas for setting your circle table: parenting books and magazines. Ask women to bring in photos of their parents. Name tag theme: your mom's and dad's first names.

like to talk about? We'll add as many of these topics as we can in our time together.

_____

_____

_____

_____

Questions from *Journal Two* our group will discuss:

❑ What are the greatest lessons you learned from your parents? How have these lessons affected your perspective as an adult?

❑ In what ways has your parents' faith strengthened your faith?

❑ Who are some of the other important adults who have influenced your growth as a child or adult? In what ways do you provide a parenting or mentoring role for children or other adults?

❑ What have you learned about parenting from God our Father?

Other topics or questions our group will discuss:

_____

_____

_____

Conversation starters: Tell us about your childhood; what is one special memory you have of time spent with your mom or dad? What do you think is an important quality in a good parent? Did this topic generate any strong feelings?

Gather in the larger circle.

Leader (optional): Would anyone like to share with us something particularly meaningful to you from your small group discussion?

Announcements, resources, reminders:

_____

_____

Comments about upcoming sessions (such as changes to group discussion topics):

Other administrative items to share with the group:

Closing prayer

Leader: Thank you for sharing with us today. Please join me in reading the closing prayer on page 47 of your journal.

Heavenly Father, thank you for all the people you have put in my life to guide my way, especially my parents. Help me truly appreciate their love and the life lessons I've learned from them, and to pass on the best of what I've received. May I always look to you as an example, loving Father. I am so grateful to be your child. Amen.

Spiritual Role Models: Martha, follower of Jesus; Gianna Beretta Molla; my personal role model

Gather into a large circle.

Opening prayer

Leader: Today's discussion helps us reflect on those people who inspire us through their example to live a Christian life.

Please join me in saying the opening prayer on page 53.

> Jesus, thank you for introducing me to your good friend Martha. Help me be a welcoming host to you and the people you bring into my life and home. Teach me to always have faith in you, even when showing my love for you is risky. Give me courage as I make decisions in my daily life, just as you gave Gianna courage throughout her life. Bring me encouragement and inspiration as I learn to recognize my spiritual role models. I will do my best to be a strong example of your love to all whose lives I touch. Amen.

Announcements or questions for the large group:

_____

_____

Instructions for dividing into small groups or pairs:

_____

_____

Group discussion

Allotted time for group discussion: _____

Ideas for setting your circle table: home and entertainment magazines, photos of Gianna and her family; books or articles about life in Jesus' time, life in Italy, or the role of rural doctors. Name tag theme: a role model in your life.

Leader: Please refer to the suggested group questions on page 63 in your journal. Before we begin our discussion, did anyone write down other questions or aspects of spiritual role models you would like to talk about? We'll add as many of these topics as we can in our time together.

_____

_____

_____

Questions from *Journal Two* our group will discuss:

☐ What about Martha's faith and action most resonates with you?

☐ In what ways does Gianna's life inspire you?

☐ Who is someone who has been a role model for you and how has that person influenced your life?

Other topics or questions our group will discuss:

_____

_____

_____

Conversation starters: What makes a good role model? When you choose role models, is it based on a specific decision they've made or how they live their lives overall? What qualities do you have that make you a good role model for someone else?

Gather in the larger circle.

Leader (optional): Would anyone like to share with us something particularly meaningful to you from your small group discussion?

Announcements, resources, reminders:

_____

_____

For our next discussion, please bring in information about or an example of a modern science or technology topic that interests you.

Comments about upcoming sessions (such as changes to group discussion topics):

_____

_____

Would anyone like to share feedback about your experience so far, either with your personal journaling or the group discussions?

Other administrative items to share with the group:

_____

_____

Closing prayer

Leader: Thank you for sharing with us today. Please join me in reading the closing prayer on pages 62-63 of your journal.

> Lord, you've shown me through Martha and Gianna and other personal role models that I can live my faith and show my love for you in my day-to-day actions, through my family, my professional life, and my community. Give me the compassion to open my heart and home as Martha did for Jesus. Grant me the courage and strength to do what's right when faced with important decisions as Gianna did. Let me be an example of your love in the way I live my life each day. Amen.

Values & Beliefs: Modern science & technology

Gather into a large circle.

Opening prayer

Leader: Today's discussion challenges us to consider how our values and beliefs help define the modern science and technology advances we use and support.

Please join me in reading the opening prayer on page 65 of your journal.

> Lord, our world is always changing. You give our best and brightest minds the ingenuity and resolve to improve our world. Guide us in our approach to research and invention. Help me make good choices about the advances I support and use in my daily life. Let me always remember to put love and human dignity in the forefront and to use the wonders of modern science and technology in ways that please you. Amen.

Announcements or questions for the large group:

_____

_____

Instructions for dividing into small groups or pairs:

_____

_____

Group discussion

Allotted time for group discussion: _____

Leader: Please refer to the suggested group questions on pages 72-73 in your journal. Before we begin our discussion, did anyone write down other questions or aspects of modern science and technology you would like to talk about? We'll add as many of these topics as we can in our time together.

_____

_____

_____

_____

Questions from *Journal Two* our group will discuss:

❑ What science and technology topics interest you the most? Which topics most challenge your beliefs? (Share information or examples brought in by women in your group.)

❑ Is there an absolute right or wrong when it comes to the creation or use of science and technology? Are there gray areas? What role does the Catholic Church play?

❑ What guidelines do you use to apply your faith values to science and technology? Does your personal involvement or need for a specific advance affect your decision?

❑ What benefits, challenges, habits, and rules does modern technology bring to your home?

Other topics or questions our group will discuss:

_____

_____

_____

Gather in the larger circle.

Leader (optional): Would anyone like to share with us something particularly meaningful to you from your small group discussion?

Conversation starters: Was this topic comfortable or difficult for you? What are some ways science and technology advances have brought good things to your life?

Announcements, resources, reminders:

_____

_____

Comments about upcoming sessions (such as changes to group
discussion topics):

_____

_____

Other administrative items to share with the group:

_____

_____

Closing prayer
Leader: Thank you for sharing with us today. Our closing prayer is
found on page 72 of your journal.

God of all creation, you give us inquisitive minds and the
ability to discover new aspects of this amazing world. Guide
us as we explore, improve, and find new ways to use nature,
technology, and our bodies. May we always respect you and
live according to your will as we choose each day to use,
support, or limit science and technology advances. Amen.

Discernment & Witnessing: Social justice— Life & dignity

Gather into a large circle.

Opening prayer

Leader: In today's discussion, we reflect on our role in social justice, especially related to the life and dignity of each person.

Please join me in reading the opening prayer on page 75 of your journal.

> Lord, you give us clear guidelines for how we are to live within our larger world. Guide me as I discern my role in supporting and promoting the principles of social justice. Grant me courage, compassion, and wisdom, and let me be a witness to all through my example. Amen.

Announcements or questions for the large group:

_____

_____

Instructions for dividing into small groups or pairs:

_____

_____

Ideas for setting your circle table: archdiocese social justice newsletter, natural family planning brochure, info about current state laws regarding life issues, related political initiatives. Name tag theme: one problem in the world you would solve today if you could wave a wand and fix it.

Group discussion

Allotted time for group discussion: _____

Leader: Please refer to the suggested group questions on pages 84-85 in your journal. Before we begin our discussion, did anyone write down other questions or aspects of social justice or life issues you would like to talk about? We'll add as many of these topics as we can in our time together.

_____

_____

_____

_____

Questions from *Journal Two* our group will discuss:

Conversation starters:
Would anyone like
to share a story
about how a life
issue has affected
you or your family?

❏   What social justice issues are closest to your heart? What questions or actions stir within you when you think about these issues? How do you or could you get involved to support these issues?

❏   How have your beliefs about life and dignity been supported or challenged in your life experience, especially related to conception, birth control, abortion, abuse, or intended death?

❏   How do you prioritize and balance one important issue over another when voting for a political candidate?

Other topics or questions our group will discuss:

_____

_____

_____

Gather in the larger circle.

Leader (optional): Would anyone like to share with us something particularly meaningful to you from your small group discussion?

Announcements, resources, reminders:

_____

_____

Comments about upcoming sessions (such as changes to group discussion topics):

_____

_____

Other administrative items to share with the group:

_____

_____

For our next discussion, please bring something that represents positive energy in your life.

Closing prayer

Leader: Thank you for sharing with us today. Please read with me our closing prayer on page 84 of your journal.

> Lord, grant me wisdom to better understand the complexities of social justice. Give me compassion, courage, and the desire to take an active role in my community to promote and improve social justice issues closest to my heart. Help me always respect and protect the life and dignity of every person, from conception through death. Amen.

Life Balance: Energy

Gather into a large circle.

Opening prayer

Leader: In today's discussion, we explore sources of physical and spiritual energy and the effect our energy level has on our ability to do God's work.

Our opening prayer is on page 87 of your journal.

> Lord, you created an amazing universe full of natural beauty and many sources of energy. Fill my heart, mind, body, and soul with energy so I may do your work each day. Help me recognize when my energy is low and guide me to springs of renewal. Amen.

Announcements or questions for the large group:

_____

_____

Instructions for dividing into small groups or pairs:

_____

_____

Group discussion

Allotted time for group discussion: _____

Leader: Please refer to the suggested group questions on page 96 in your journal. Before we begin our discussion, did anyone write down other questions or aspects of energy you would like to talk about? We'll add as many of these topics as we can in our time together.

_____

_____

_____

Questions from *Journal Two* our group will discuss:

❏ How do you feel about your overall energy level? What energizes you and what drains you of your energy physically or emotionally? How do your environment, work, and the people in your life affect your energy?

❏ What does spiritual energy mean to you? Why do we need it? How does your spiritual energy affect your trust in God?

❏ What do you believe about how God enters our hearts? How has the Spirit worked through you or others close to you?

Other topics or questions our group will discuss:

_____

_____

_____

Conversation starters: Who are some of the people in your life or what activities give you good energy? How do you know when your spiritual energy is low?

Gather in the larger circle.

Leader (optional): Would anyone like to share with us something particularly meaningful to you from your small group discussion?

Announcements, resources, reminders:

_____

_____

*Do participants
need to bring
anything for your
final session based
on the format you
have chosen?*

Comments about the final session (which format have you chosen and how will it work?):

_____

_____

Other administrative items to share with the group:

_____

_____

Closing prayer

Leader: Thank you for sharing with us today. Please read with me our closing prayer on page 95 of your journal.

Holy Spirit, fill me with love and energy so my light may shine brightly. Help me make good choices about my environment, work, and the people I spend time with so that I fill my day with and share positive energy. I recognize my need for both physical and spiritual energy in my life. Grant me the courage to trust you and to allow you to enter my heart to reach others and do God's will. Amen.

 # Reflections

The final chapter in the journal is a way to bring together the whole experience and for each woman to reflect on what she has learned about herself and how this experience will impact her life.

Following are three different types of final meetings. Select the format that seems best suited to your group. You can always modify it to meet your needs. Option one is similar to the previous sessions, using the chapter-ending questions. Option two is a social gathering, with the focus on sharing resources and talking informally about what each person liked best about the experience and the ways it has changed her perspective. Option three is a more reflective session that includes a review of each chapter.

Our group will follow this option for our final session: _____

Option One: Small group discussions
Gather into a large circle.

Opening prayer
Leader: Today we reflect on this experience we've shared together and how it has and will impact our lives. Please join me in reading the opening prayer on page 99 of your journal.

> Lord, thank you for the circle of women you have brought into my life. Thank you for the time and opportunity to reflect on the topics in this journal. Help me continue to carve out time in my week to reflect on ways I live my faith in my daily life. Encourage me to develop an intimate relationship with you, to create personal rituals and habits that are loving and giving, to let the wisdom and love of my parents guide my actions as an adult, to put lessons from my spiritual role models into action, to make good choices about my use and support of modern science and technology advances, to honor and respect all life, and to fill my heart, mind, body, and soul with positive energy so that I may do your work each day. Amen.

Announcements or questions for the large group:

_____

_____

Instructions for dividing into small groups or pairs:

_____

_____

Group discussion

Allotted time for group discussion: _____

Leader: Please refer to the suggested group questions on pages 104-105 in your journal.

Questions from *Journal Two* our group will discuss:

❑ What is one thing you learned about yourself or your faith during this time of journaling?

❑ What is one thing you are now inspired to change? Or one thing you are currently doing that has been affirmed by this experience?

❑ What aspect of this experience did you enjoy the most? The time you spent with yourself reflecting and journaling? The fellowship with other women? Something else?

❑ You have been exploring how you live your faith in your daily life. In what ways would you like to take that exploration a step further? Is there a topic that resonated with you or a new topic you thought of while journaling that you would like to learn more about? What will you look for next in your spiritual journey?

❑ Do you have resources you'd like to share with the group or a resource you are looking for?

Gather in a large circle. Refer to the closing on page 44 of this guide.

Option Two: Social gathering

Before your meeting, prepare a table of resources and table for refreshments. Ask women to bring in a snack and a resource to share.

Gather into a large circle.

Opening prayer

Leader: Today we celebrate the friendships created in our circle and share how this experience has and will impact our lives. Please join me in reading the opening prayer on page 99 of your journal.

> Lord, thank you for the circle of women you have brought into my life. Thank you for the time and opportunity to reflect on the topics in this journal. Help me continue to carve out time in my week to reflect on ways I live my faith in my daily life. Encourage me to develop an intimate relationship with you, to create personal rituals and habits that are loving and giving, to let the wisdom and love of my parents guide my actions as an adult, to put lessons from my spiritual role models into action, to make good choices about my use and support of modern science and technology advances, to honor and respect all life, and to fill my heart, mind, body, and soul with positive energy so that I may do your work each day. Amen.

Leader: Would anyone like to share information about a resource you brought with you today? (Allow time for sharing.) While you browse the resource table and enjoy the refreshments, I encourage you to share with each other what you enjoyed about this experience, the ways you feel changed by it, and what you think might be next steps on your spiritual journey.

Direct the women to the resource and refreshment tables. Toward the end of your meeting time, gather again in your large circle and refer to the closing on page 44 of this guide.

Option Three: Review and reflection

This option includes time for individual reflection, sharing with partners, and small group discussion. Create an intimate atmosphere that, if possible, is slightly different from what you have been using and that allows for both personal quiet time and small group discussion. Participants can bring a blanket and pillow to relax on the floor or you can set up chairs in a circle.

Light candles in the center of the room and turn down the lights. Play soft music in the background. Gather in a large circle around the "campfire" of candles.

Opening prayer

Open with light relaxation exercises and a prayer, such as:

(*Leader guides the group, reading slowly with a relaxed voice.*)

Stand an arm's length apart. Close your eyes if you'd like.

Spread your arms, open your chest, and breathe in deep, filling your lungs. Pushing your arms forward, push out all the stale air until your lungs are empty. Continue breathing in and out in deep breaths.

Breathe in love and positive thoughts.

Breathe out all negativity and stress.

Breathe in comfort, understanding, and forgiveness.

Breathe out pain, hurt, and misunderstandings.

Breathe in peace and calm, more love and trust.

Breathe out all of the to-do lists, all the worries of the day.

Bring your hands to your heart center in prayer.

Lord, thank you for the time and opportunity to reflect on the topics in this journal. Help each of us open our hearts to listen and follow where you lead.

Leader: Please sit comfortably and we'll take a few moments to reflect on each chapter.

Chapter reflections

Select one or two leaders to quietly read the following summary statements and reflective questions to the group. There is no discussion; this is a time to give each person a chance to reflect in her own mind what she has discovered about herself in recent weeks. Pause after each question to allow a moment of reflection.

Leader reads:

Connecting with God: Spiritual intimacy & inspiration
Recognizing the challenges and joys of our other intimate relationships can help us build a closer relationship with God.

How do I nurture my intimate relationships?

What does my ideal relationship with God feel like?

What sources of inspiration can help me gain perspective and encourage me to get to know God better and grow closer to him?

Rituals & Traditions: Personal rituals & routines
Being purposeful in our rituals and routines helps us bring joy to our relationships, support our own spiritual growth, and provide a sense of belonging and safety for the special people in our lives.

What signs of love and affection do I most enjoy giving or receiving?

How have my rituals and routines with family or friends helped me build loving and lasting relationships?

How do my personal habits limit or encourage my spiritual growth?

Relationships: Parents
Our parents are our first teachers. Through their actions and example, parents help us develop our sense of self and our place within our larger society.

What are the greatest lessons I learned from my parents and other important adults in my life?

How do I influence the lives of other children and adults?

What qualities of God as Father do I most want to emulate?

Spiritual Role Models: Martha; Gianna Beretta Molla; personal
Martha, one of Christ's first evangelists, invited Jesus into her life
even when it caused her more work and even when it was risky.
Gianna carried out her beliefs in her profession and community, and
risked her life for her unborn child.

How do the actions of Martha and Gianna encourage me to live my
faith and make the right choices?

Who in my life has made a courageous decision?

How do my actions and decisions set an example for others?

Values & Beliefs: Modern science & technology
Advances in science, medicine, and technology improve our world
but come with a responsibility to create and use them according to
God's laws.

What science and technology topics challenge my beliefs?

How do I choose which advances to use, support, or limit?

Does my personal need for a specific advance affect my decision?

Discernment & Witnessing: Social justice—Life & dignity
Social justice principles guide how we as a society provide for each
person's needs, the foundation being the sacredness of human life.

How have my beliefs about conception, birth control, abortion,
abuse, or intended death been supported or challenged in my life?

What role do I play in social justice? How can I make a difference?

Life Balance: Energy
Our physical and spiritual energy directly affects our ability to do
God's work.

What aspects of my life positively or negatively affect my energy?

How does renewing my spiritual energy help me consciously open
my heart to God and do God's work?

Partner sharing

Leader: Turn and face a partner. Take five minutes for one person to answer the following question while your partner listens. Then take five minutes for the second partner to answer the same question.

What is one thing you learned about yourself or your faith during this time of journaling?

Leader: Now turn in the other direction and face a new partner. Each partner answers:

What is one thing you are now inspired to change? Or one thing you are currently doing that has been affirmed by this experience?

Small group campfires

Split participants into small groups of four to seven people, with each group encircling one of the candle campfires. Ask the women to share with their group answers to the following questions (from pp. 104-105 in the journal) or other questions that you've decided beforehand.

What aspect of this experience did you enjoy the most? The time you spent with yourself reflecting and journaling? The fellowship with other women? Something else?

You have been exploring how you live your faith in your daily life. In what ways would you like to take that exploration a step further? Is there a topic that resonated with you or a new topic you thought of while journaling that you would like to learn more about? What will you look for next in your spiritual journey?

Do you have resources you'd like to share with the group or a resource you are looking for?

Large group closing *(same for all three options)*
Invite participants to come in close together in a circle around the
candle(s). Bring up the lights if needed.

Leader: Please read with me the petition of thanks on page 105 of
your journal:

> Lord, thank you for the circle of women you have brought
> into my life. Thank you for encouraging me to take this time
> for myself. Thank you for guiding me on my personal
> journey.

Leader: I invite you to offer your own additional petition of thanks.
(Pause to allow petitions from anyone who wishes to share.)

Leader: Together as a group let's read the poem "In the Circle" on the
last page of your journal as our final closing prayer.

Closing prayer

In the Circle

I find myself
in the circle
having walked an open path

around and round
in peacefulness
within a labyrinth

with each step
my joys and tears
with other women shared

burdens lifted
on the journey
to the center where

I find myself
in the circle
I did not walk alone

sitting with me
here the Father
the Spirit, and the Son

together we
will journey out
a path I know so well

renewed in faith
with strength and love
I found here in the circle

Retreats

*Throughout your
weekend, be
sure to add
opportunities
for laughter,
music, and time
for women to get
to know each
other socially.*

The *Circle of Catholic Women* journal and facilitator guide is primarily set up to accommodate a weekly journaling program. Most suggestions in the journal assume that participants will have a week or so to journal independently and privately reflect on a topic before sharing in a group discussion. However, the *Circle of Catholic Women* program can easily be adapted to a retreat format as well.

Retreats can take many forms, including half-day and full-day retreats, weekend retreats, and multi-day parish missions. Following are suggestions for using the journal in a retreat setting.

Retreat theme

Define a theme for your retreat. Your theme can be as broad as helping women find balance in their lives or as specific as exploring the life of a particular spiritual role model.

Consider how the individual topics within *Journal Two* complement and support your theme. Which topics most closely match? What additional information could be presented along with the journaling to help participants delve deeper into the topic and discussion?

The weekend retreat

Divide your retreat time into blocks of no more than 60 to 90 minutes to keep attention spans fresh. Select up to three journal topics for each half day of retreat time. The following is a sample schedule for a weekend retreat using several topics from the journal. For the presentation portion, you can use readings and information from the journal or supplement with photos, videos, guest speakers, or additional information about the topic. Especially when retreat participants have not had an opportunity to read the journal chapters before the retreat, the presentation portion gives them an opportunity to become engaged in the topic and begin to reflect on it before discussing with their small groups. A sample activity is given for one afternoon session. You can create similar activities throughout the weekend to help keep participants engaged and to break up the time sitting, listening, and talking.

Seat participants around small tables. Throughout the retreat, use a combination of large group presentations and small group discussions. Encourage participants to change seats at each break or meal time to get to know other participants and hear new perspectives. As much as is practical, include the concepts of circles and labyrinths and encourage prayerful personal reflection.

Friday evening

7:00 PM   Arrive for social gathering. Ice-breaker activities. Receive journals and retreat materials.

7:30   Presentation on spiritual intimacy: intimate relationships, spiritual practices that bring us closer to God.

8:00   Participants journal about their special relationships and sources of spiritual inspiration.

Saturday

8:00 AM   Breakfast with small group discussion. Each person at the table shares her favorite source of spiritual inspiration. Discussion: What does it mean to be intimate with God? What is your ideal relationship with God?

9:00-9:20   Large group presentation on parenting. What does God
             expect from parents? From children? How can the
             lessons we learn from our parents help us to be good
             Christians throughout our lives?

9:20-10:00   Small group discussion. Our parents are our first
             teachers. What are the greatest lessons you learned from
             your parents and other important adults in your life?
             What parenting or mentoring roles help you influence
             the lives of other children or adults? What can we learn
             from God as our Father?

10:00-10:20 Break

10:20-10:40 Role models. Presentation on Martha, follower of Jesus;
            and Gianna Beretta Molla.

10:40-11:30 Small group discussion. In what ways can you look to
            Martha or Gianna as an inspiration for your life? How are
            you a good host like Martha; in what ways are you
            distracted from spending time with Jesus? Who in your
            life has made a courageous decision like Gianna? When
            you choose role models, is it based on a specific
            decision they've made or how they live their lives
            overall? How does Gianna's example in her professional
            life and community inspire you to take action and live
            your faith in your work and neighborhood? Are you a
            role model? How do your actions or decisions inspire or
            provide an example for others?

11:30-12:30 Lunch. Browse resource table. Time for personal
            reflection or journaling about the morning topics.

12:30-1:00 Large group presentation on the key principles of social
            justice, with examples of issues as well as programs that
            help solve the issue. The sacredness of life and human
            dignity form the foundation underlying these principles.

1:00-1:50   Life and dignity activity. Write out several situations that
             involve personal decisions related to life and dignity.
             Give each small group one of the situation descriptions.
             In small groups, consider the situation and discuss the
             questions. Then share responses with the larger group.

Examples of situations that touch on conception, birth control,
abortion, abuse, and end of life:

You and your husband have been unsuccessful in conceiving. You've
tried every natural means you've read about and learned from your
doctor. You've prayed and feel that God is calling you to be parents.
Your doctor gives you information about in vitro fertilization.

You and your husband have five children. God has always provided,
but it's getting more difficult to financially support your family. Your
last two pregnancies came unexpectedly while using natural family
planning. Your best friend asks if you're going to consider other
forms of birth control.

You are a 47-year-old woman who was recently raped. You just found
out you are pregnant as a result. Your doctor has presented abortion
as an option for you to consider due to risks associated with having
a baby at your age as well as psychological effects of the rape.

Your sister and her two children are staying the night with you after
her husband physically abused her. She insists her bruises do not
need medical attention and she plans to return home after her
husband "cools off."

Your mother has neared the end of her battle with terminal cancer.
She is ready to die and has asked to receive enough pain killer to
help her go to sleep peacefully for the last time.

Sample questions for the small group:
What does Catholic social teaching say to do in this situation?
Consider first that you are the person in the situation. What options

49

do you consider? What are your strongest feelings? Fears? Comforts? Now imagine you are a professional involved. How do you guide this person? If you are a friend, family member, or neighbor who wants to help, what action do you take?

Which was more challenging, facing the situation yourself or trying to help? Did you follow the Church teachings? Why or why not? What made it easy or difficult to decide? (Share with large group.)

1:50-2:20 Small group discussion. How have your beliefs about life and dignity been supported or challenged in your own personal life experience? What do you consider your role to be in social justice? How can you make a difference beyond your personal choices? What social justice issues are closest to your heart? How do you prioritize and balance one important issue over another when selecting the organizations you support or when voting for a political candidate?

2:20-2:40 Break

2:40-3:00 Large group discussion on science and technology. Advances in science, medicine, and technology improve our world but come with a responsibility to create and use them according to God's laws.

3:00-3:30 Small group discussion. What science and technology topics challenge your beliefs? How do you choose which advances to use, support, or limit? Does your personal need for a specific advance affect your decision?

3:30-4:00 Small group discussion about personal habits. Being purposeful about our rituals and routines helps us bring joy to our relationships, support our own spiritual growth, and provide a sense of belonging and safety for the special people in our lives. Think about your typical day, especially times of transition (morning, after school/work, bedtime). What rules or routines help make your day positive? Describe some of the special rituals or routines your family or friends can count on that help you build loving relationships. What signs of love and affection do you most enjoy giving or receiving? How do your personal habits limit or encourage your spiritual growth?

4:00-5:00   Optional labyrinth walk. Set up a labyrinth and prayer area for participants to spend time in prayer and reflection. Participants may alternately use this time for exercise or social activities. Some groups also provide an option to participate in crafts or charitable activities.

5:00-6:30   Dinner

7:00-9:00   Optional energy session (see Sunday morning), prayer service, time for personal journaling, or group entertainment.

Sunday morning
8:00 AM   Mass

9:00   Breakfast

9:30-9:50   Energy. Write down as many things (people, places, activities, etc.) you can think of that energize you. Then make a list of those things that drain your energy. Which do you spend more time with each day? What changes in your physical environment or the activities or people you spend time with could bring you more positive energy?

9:50-10:30 Small group discussion. What is spiritual energy? Why do we need it? How is it similar or different from our physical energy? How can the sources of spiritual inspiration we talked about at the beginning of the retreat renew your spiritual energy?

51

10:30-10:45 Break

10:45-11:30 Wrap up. Encourage participants to spend time with their journals over the next two months as a way to continue to personally reflect on these topics and go a level deeper in their journey. Suggest journaling about one topic each week. Ask reflective questions for them to consider, such as: What stories did you hear this weekend that helped change your perspective or that inspired you to look deeper at your faith? Were there topics that were difficult for you to discuss? Consider spending more time with those.

Retreat facilitators might also want to use the reflective questions from pages 41-44 of this facilitator guide as a wrapup to your retreat.

Closing prayer

Lord, thank you for the blessing of this circle of women. Thank you for encouraging us to take this time together and for guiding each of us on our journey.

Read together the poem on the last page of the journal (p. 45 of this facilitator guide).

Alternate retreat formats and ideas

There are many possible variations on the previous retreat format. A few ideas:

Select one or two chapters only and focus the retreat on that topic. Add more activities, physical exercises, and events around the topic. For example, you could hold a social justice fair to introduce women to local programs or spend an afternoon or evening serving through one of the programs. Ask a scientist to talk about progress being made toward medical cures as a result of ethical research. Take a hike to a nearby lake or mountain as a source of spiritual inspiration.

Register participants a month or two before the retreat and ask them to journal about the retreat topics leading up to the retreat. Set up the retreat as a "journey" with each topic in a different room. Decorate each room with table objects and resources for that topic. Split your retreat audience into multiple small groups and hold simultaneous sessions in each room. Each hour switch to a new room and topic.

Focus the retreat on individual reflection and allow for personal journaling time within the retreat schedule. Arrange labyrinth walks and quiet places for individual prayer and reflection. Schedule times for nature walks, music, yoga, meditation, and penance services. Bring the group together once or twice to reflect on a topic and share journaling experiences from the weekend.

Spread out the journal topics over the course of the school year. Meet once a month for two hours. Bring in guest speakers to discuss the month's topic in more depth. Ask participants to journal about the topic over the course of the previous month. After listening to the speaker, participants can talk in small groups about their journaling experience, the speaker's insight, and new perspectives they've gained over the month.

Retreat planner
Use the following pages to write out your thoughts and plan the retreat that meets the needs of your circle.

Retreat theme(s):

_____

Days/times available for retreat:

Date: _____   From: _____ AM/PM   To: _____ AM/PM

Date: _____   From: _____ AM/PM   To: _____ AM/PM

Date: _____   From: _____ AM/PM   To: _____ AM/PM

Will participants journal before, during or after the retreat?

Journal topics to include and portions of the topic(s) or questions we'll use from the journal:

Topic _____   Pages _____

Topic _____   Pages _____

Topic _____   Pages _____

Topic _____   Pages _____

Topic _____   Pages _____

Topic _____   Pages _____

Topic _____   Pages _____

Topic _____   Pages _____

Additional activities or information we'll add for these topics:

_____

_____

_____

_____

_____

Draft schedule:

_____

_____

_____

_____

_____

_____

_____

_____

_____

_____

Conveniences, food, parking, and other details needed:

_____

_____

_____

_____

Location options:

_____

_____

_____

Retreat coordinators, speakers, and facilitators needed:

_____

_____

_____

_____

Supplies, props, decorations, presentations, resources needed:

_____

_____

_____

_____

Draft of retreat announcement and marketing/publicity ideas:

_____

_____

_____

_____

Additional planning items:

_____

_____

_____

_____

_____

Continuing the Circle

Feedback

No matter which format you choose for your program, consider giving the women in your group the opportunity to provide feedback on their experience. A survey or other feedback can help you improve the program to better meet the needs of your parish, women's ministry, or community. It also lets the women who participated have a voice to let you know what they loved or didn't.

In addition to inviting feedback throughout the program, consider asking the women in your group to complete a written survey that they return by mail or email. Collect feedback within two weeks of the event or program end so the feedback is fresh in the participants' minds. Give an option to provide a name or remain anonymous.

Areas you might ask about on the feedback survey include level of satisfaction with the location, schedule, facilitation, journal topics, and overall experience. Invite additional comments and suggestions. Ask about the person's interest in similar future events and if she would recommend the program to a friend.

Post-program gathering

Often when women participate in a circle program, foundations of friendship form with other women in the circle along with a desire to continue those relationships. Consider a social gathering a month or so after the program. This can be a simple evening of games and refreshments, a prayer breakfast with a guest speaker, or an informal gathering at someone's home with a chance to catch up on what has happened since the group last met.

Some groups continue to meet for breakfast once a month to share experiences on their journey and to continue nurturing friendships. Some participate in outreach programs together. Others fold their circle into a larger women's ministry organization.

Alternating circle journals with other programs

Many parishes host adult enrichment programs throughout the year. Look at your offerings for women. Is there a place in the schedule for an annual retreat or weekly journaling session? The *Circle of Catholic Women* journal series is nonsequential so women can join a new journal at any time. Consider alternating a circle journal program with a book or Bible study and Lenten faith sharing program. Or consider hosting a fall or spring retreat. Alternating programs gives women a chance to take a break from one format and to enrich their faith in multiple ways. It also helps women new to the group feel welcome and helps accommodate busy schedules throughout the year.

Circle outreach

The circle program was created to help women deepen their faith and find balance in their everyday lives. With renewed spiritual balance many women find a greater desire to give back to their communities. If you don't already have a women's ministry outreach program, consider organizing a few events with this circle. If possible, select programs that allow the women in your circle, along with their families if desired, to participate in hands-on programs that benefit other women and families. For example, our women's ministry began with a Mother's Day event at a local homeless shelter. Upstairs, women from our group gave manicures and served popcorn and soda while the parents staying at the shelter enjoyed a movie. Downstairs, other women and older children from our group played with the children at the shelter. Our children were able to see that these children were very much like themselves except that their bedrooms were behind the cardboard privacy screens at the edges of the room and all of their belongings could fit into one bag. One of us took photos of each child with a digital camera and printed the photos onsite for a scrapbook. Each child created a mini-scrapbook with their photo, Bible verses, and drawings. We brought donated bath items and the children picked out a basket of items for their moms and dads. At the end of the evening, the children gave the baskets and scrapbooks as gifts to their parent(s). The event was simple to plan and gave each family a wonderful evening and a special gift. It lifted our spirits as much as theirs.

Other ideas include sorting clothes at a local thrift shop, wrapping and delivering holiday gifts to families in need, delivering meals or Eucharist to the elderly or ill, serving lunch at a local soup kitchen, or distributing food at a local food shelter.

Check with your pastor, pastoral care or social justice team, or local Catholic Charities office for information about family outreach programs in your area.

Outreach programs that might interest our circle of women:

_____

_____

_____

_____

_____

Custom circle programs

If your group would like help planning a circle program or retreat or need a custom program with specific topics not currently included in one of the *Circle of Catholic Women* journals, please contact staff@circleofcatholicwomen.com. The web site www.circleofcatholicwomen.com is also a great place to share ideas that have worked for your circle with other Catholic women around the world.

Many blessings as you lead the women in your circle to deepen their faith and find balance in their everyday lives. Together may we all journey to the center.

God bless.